How to Start a YouTube Channel for Fun & Profit 2024 Edition: The Ultimate Guide

CRYSTAL BOWEN

DEDICATION

To all the dreamers and doers out there this one's for you. May your passion shine through every video and your creativity inspire millions? Thank you for believing in your voice and sharing your unique story with the world. Here's to your YouTube journey let's make some magic together

CONTENTS

ACKNOWLEDGMENTS

Creating "How to Start a YouTube Channel for Fun & Profit 2024 Edition: The Ultimate Guide" has been an incredible journey, and it wouldn't have been possible without the support of so many amazing people.

First and foremost, I want to thank almighty God and thank you to my family and friends for their unwavering encouragement and patience while I immersed myself in this project. Your belief in me kept me going, even on the toughest days.

To my fellow YouTubers and the incredible community of creators your passion, creativity, and generosity have inspired every page of this book. Special shoutout to those who shared their insights and experiences with me you know who you are. This book is as much yours as it is mine.

To my readers and future YouTube stars, thank you for choosing this guide as your companion on your journey. Your dreams and ambitions are what make this work meaningful. Remember, every big YouTuber started with zero subscribers, just like you.

Lastly, to the team at Amazon KDP, thanks for providing a platform that make sharing this knowledge possible.

Here's to creating, sharing, and thriving together on YouTube. Let's make some magic happen!

CHAPTER 1
Affirmations for a Successful YouTube Journey

- I am becoming a successful YouTuber, one video at a time.
- My content connects with my audience in meaningful ways.
- I attract loyal subscribers who enjoy and support my work.
- My creativity and passion are evident in every video I create.
- I feel confident and authentic when I'm on camera.
- My channel is growing steadily, and I'm excited about the journey.
- I provide real value and inspiration to my viewers.
- I'm committed to constantly improving my skills and content.
- I see challenges as opportunities to grow and learn.
- My videos are reaching and impacting more people every day.
- I am a positive influence within the YouTube community.
- My audience eagerly awaits my new content.
- I work well with other creators and enjoy collaborating.
- My channel is starting to generate a solid income.
- I balance creativity with smart strategies effortlessly.
- I'm always learning and keeping up with new trends.
- My voice and message are strong and clear.
- I genuinely enjoy creating content and engaging with my audience.
- I am thankful for the platform and the community I've built.
- I inspire others to follow their passions through my journey.

CHAPTER 2
How to Start a YouTube Channel: A Step-by-Step Guide

<u>Setting Up Your Channel</u>

Create a Google Account: If you don't already have one, create a Google account.

Set up Your YouTube Channel: Go to YouTube, sign in with your Google account, and follow the prompts to set up your channel.

Customize Your Channel: Add a profile picture, banner, and channel description to make your channel visually appealing and informative.

<u>Creating Your First Video</u>

Choose Your Topic: Pick a topic that aligns with your niche and audience.

Plan Content: Outline the main points and structure of your video.

Record Video: Use a good quality camera and microphone to ensure clear visuals and audio.

<u>Uploading and Optimizing Content</u>

Upload Your Video: Follow YouTube's guidelines for uploading your video.

Optimize Title and Description: Use relevant keywords in your title and description to improve search ability.

Add Tags and Thumbnails: Use tags related to your content and create an eye-catching thumbnail.

<u>Video Editing Tools</u>

DaVinci Resolve

Powerful video editing software with advanced features for color correction and audio post production.

Website: DaVinci Resolve

Shotcut;

An open source, cross platform video editor that supports a wide range of formats.

Website: Shotcut

OpenShot

A simple, user-friendly video editor that's great for beginners.

Website: OpenShot

Thumbnail Creation Tools

Canva

A graphic design tool with pre-made templates for YouTube thumbnails.

Website: Canva

Pixlr

A free online photo editor with powerful editing features.

Website: Pixlr

Snappa

A graphic design tool with templates specifically for YouTube thumbnails.

Audio Editing Tools

Audacity

An open-source, cross-platform audio editor that's perfect for recording and editing audio.

Website: Audacity

Ocenaudio

A user-friendly audio editor with real-time effects and cross-platform support.

Website: Ocenaudio

CHAPTER 3
: Five Steps to Become a Successful YouTuber

Step 1: Identifying your niche and target Audience

Choose a topic or niche that you are passionate about. This could be anything from gaming, beauty, tech reviews, cooking, education, travel, or fitness. Your enthusiasm for the subject will shine through in your videos and keep you motivated.

Understand the current landscape of your chosen niche. Look at what other creators are doing, identify gaps in the content, and find your unique angle. This will help you stand out from the competition.

Determine who your ideal viewers are. Consider their age, gender, interests, and what kind of content they enjoy. Creating a detailed viewer persona can help tailor your content to meet their needs and preferences.

Once your niche and target audience are identified, ensure your content consistently aligns with these elements. This helps in building a loyal subscriber base that knows what to expect from your channel.

Step 2: Develop high-quality content

Plan your videos ahead of time. Create a content calendar to organize your ideas and ensure a consistent upload schedule. This helps in managing your time and maintaining consistency.

Write scripts or outlines for your videos to stay on track and convey your message clearly. Storyboarding can help visualize the video flow and ensure smooth transitions between segments.

Invest in good-quality equipment, including a camera, microphone, and lighting. A high production value can significantly impact viewers and subscribers. Ensure your audio is clear and your video is well-lit and visually appealing.

Step 3: Optimize for Search Engine Optimization (SEO)

Use tools like Google Trends, YouTube's search bar, and keyword research tools to find popular and relevant keywords in your niche. Incorporate these keywords naturally into your video titles, descriptions, and tags.

Create eye-catching and informative titles that include your primary keywords. Your title should give a clear idea of what the video is about while enticing viewers to click.

Write detailed video descriptions that provide more contexts about your content. Include keywords naturally, and add links to relevant videos, your social media, and any other resources.

Use tags to help YouTube understand the content and context of your video. Include a mix of broad and specific tags to reach a wider audience. Choose the appropriate category for your video to enhance its discoverability.

Create customized thumbnails that are visually appealing and relevant to the video content. Thumbnails should have bright colors, clear images, and readable text to stand out in search results.

Step 4: Engage with Your Community

Engage with your viewers and subscribers by responding to their comments. This shows that you value their input and helps build a community around your channel.

Encourage viewers and subscribers to leave feedback and suggestions in the comments. This can provide valuable insights into what your audience likes and what you can improve.

Promote your YouTube content on other social media platforms. Interact with your followers on these platforms to build a broader community.

Step 5: Consistently analyze and improve

Regularly review your YouTube analytics to understand how your videos are performing. Pay attention to metrics such as watch time, audience retention, click-through rates, and subscriber growth.

You should be open to feedback and willing to adapt your content strategy based on your analysis. Continuous improvement is key to staying relevant and growing your channel.

Keep up with the latest trends and updates on YouTube. The platform's algorithms and features can change, and staying informed will help you adapt and optimize your content strategy effectively.

CHAPTER 4
Legal and Ethical Considerations

As you embark on your YouTube journey, it's essential to keep legal and ethical considerations at the forefront. Navigating these aspects can seem daunting, but it's crucial for maintaining your channel's integrity and ensuring its long-term success. Let's break down some of the key points you need to be aware of, in a way that's straightforward and human.

Copyright Issues
Understanding Copyright:

When you use someone else's work, such as music, images, or video clips, without permission, you could be infringing on their copyright. This can lead to videos being taken down, or worse, legal action.

To avoid this, make sure you have the right to use the content. This might mean using royalty-free music, purchasing a license, or creating original content.

Creative Commons:

Some creators allow their work to be used for free under a Creative Commons license. Be sure to read the terms of the license, as some may require attribution or restrict commercial use.

YouTube's Audio Library:

Take advantage of YouTube's free Audio Library, which offers music and sound effects that you can safely use in your videos.

Privacy Concerns

Respecting Privacy:

Always respect the privacy of others. If you're filming in public, be mindful of who might be in your footage. Obtaining permission is a good practice, especially if someone is a prominent part of your video.

Avoid sharing personal information about others without their consent. This includes names, addresses, and any other identifiable information.

Minors in Videos:

If your content features minors, make sure you have explicit permission from their parents or guardians. Be extra cautious about the type of content you are producing to ensure it's appropriate and respectful.

Compliance with YouTube Policies
Community Guidelines:

Familiarize yourself with YouTube's community guidelines. These rules are in place to keep the platform safe and enjoyable for everyone. They cover areas like hate speech, harassment, and harmful content.

Violating these guidelines can lead to your videos being removed, and repeated violations can result in your channel being suspended or banned.

Monetization Policies:

If you plan to monetize your content, understand YouTube's monetization policies. This includes adhering to guidelines about what types of content are eligible for ads. YouTube is strict about this, as advertisers want their ads to appear on appropriate and high-quality content.

Ethical Considerations
Authenticity and Honesty:

Be authentic and honest with your audience. If you're reviewing products, give your genuine opinion. Transparency builds trust, and trust is crucial for a loyal audience.

Disclose any sponsorships or partnerships. If you're being paid to promote a product, let your viewers know. Not only is this a legal requirement in many places, but it also helps maintain your credibility.

Responsibility to Your Audience:

Recognize the influence you have as a content creator. Your words and actions can impact your viewers, so strive to be a positive role model. Promote respectful behavior and discourage negativity or harmful actions.

Be mindful of the content you produce, especially if your audience includes younger viewers. Avoid promoting unsafe practices or misinformation.

Handling Negative Feedback:

Learn to handle criticism professionally. Not all feedback will be positive, and that's okay. Responding calmly and constructively to negative comments can show maturity and dedication to improving your channel.

If you encounter harassment or abusive comments, use YouTube's tools to report and manage such behavior. You have the right to maintain a positive environment on your channel.

By staying informed and conscientious about these legal and ethical aspects, you can protect yourself and your channel while building a reputable and trustworthy presence on YouTube. It's not just about avoiding trouble; it's about creating a positive and respectful community where your content can thrive.

CHAPTER 5
Analytics and performance tracking

Understanding how your videos perform is crucial to growing your YouTube channel. Analytics provide you with the data you need to make informed decisions about your content and strategy. Here's how you can leverage YouTube Analytics to improve your channel's performance in a way that's easy to understand and act upon.

Why Analytics Matter

Analytics give you insights into your audience's behavior, preferences, and engagement. They tell you what's working, what's not, and where you can improve. By paying attention to these metrics, you can tailor your content to better meet your audience's needs, which helps grow your channel.

Key Metrics to Monitor

Watch Time: This is the total amount of time viewers spend watching your videos. It's one of the most important metrics because YouTube's algorithm prioritizes videos with higher watch times. The longer people watch your videos, the more likely YouTube is to recommend them to others.

Average View Duration: This tells you the average length of time viewers spend watching your video. If viewers consistently watch your videos for a long duration, it indicates that your content is engaging and holding their attention.

Audience Retention: This metric shows you how well your video retains viewers over time. It's usually represented as a graph that drops off as viewers leave the video. High audience retention means people are watching your videos almost to the end, which is a good signal to YouTube.

Click-Through Rate (CTR): CTR measures how often people click on your video after seeing the thumbnail and title. A high CTR means your title and thumbnail are effective at grabbing attention. If your CTR is low, you might need to improve your thumbnails or make your titles more compelling.

Engagement Metrics: These include likes, dislikes, comments, and shares. High engagement indicates that viewers are interacting with your content, which can boost your video's visibility and help build a community around your channel.

Subscriber Growth: Keep track of how many new subscribers you gain over a certain period. This metric shows you how well you're content is converting viewers into subscribers.

How to Use This Data

Identify popular content: Look at which videos have the highest watch time, retention, and engagement. These are the videos that your audience loves the most. Use this information to guide your future content creation. Make more of what works and less of what doesn't.

Improve underperforming videos: For videos with low watch time or high drop-off rates, analyze the content to see what might be causing viewers to leave. It could be the length, pacing, or even the topic. Experiment with different approaches based on this feedback.

Optimize Thumbnails and Titles: If your CTR is low, try testing different thumbnails and titles. Make sure they are eye-catching and accurately represent the content of the video. A/B testing can be useful here; try different variations and see which performs better.

Engage with your audience: Respond to comments and encourage viewers to like, share, and subscribe. High engagement not only boosts your video's ranking in YouTube's algorithm but also helps build a loyal community.

Regularly review analytics: Make it a habit to check your analytics regularly. Weekly or monthly reviews can help you stay on top of your channel's performance and make timely adjustments to your strategy.

Adapt and grow: YouTube is constantly evolving, and so should your strategy. Stay informed about new features and changes in the algorithm. Be flexible and willing to adapt based on what the data tells you.

By understanding and utilizing YouTube Analytics, you can make data-driven decisions that enhance your content and grow your channel. It's all about knowing what your audience loves and delivering more of it while continuously learning and improving along the way.

CHAPTER 6
Understanding the YouTube Algorithm

The YouTube algorithm can seem like a complex and mysterious force, but understanding how it works is crucial for growing your channel. The algorithm determines which videos are suggested to viewers, what shows up in search results, and which videos get featured on the homepage. Here's a more human-friendly explanation of how you can navigate and leverage the YouTube algorithm to your advantage.

How the Algorithm Works
User Behavior: The algorithm prioritizes content based on user behavior. This includes what videos users watch, what they like, comment on, share, and how long they watch a video. Essentially, the more engaged a viewer is with your content, the more likely the algorithm is to recommend your videos to others.

Watch Time: Watch time is one of the most important factors. It measures how long viewers stay on your video and YouTube overall. The platform aims to keep users engaged for as long as possible, so videos that contribute to longer watch times are favored. This means creating content that captures and holds the viewer's attention is key.

Click-Through Rate (CTR): Your video's thumbnail and title play a huge role in attracting clicks. The CTR is calculated by the number of people who click on your video divided by the number of people who see it. Eye-catching thumbnails and compelling titles that accurately represent your content can significantly boost your CTR.

Engagement: Likes, comments, shares, and subscriptions are all forms of engagement that the algorithm takes into account. When viewers interact with your video, it signals to YouTube that your content is engaging and worth promoting to a wider audience.

Consistency: Regularly uploading content helps keep your channel active in the eyes of both your audience and the algorithm. Consistent posting schedules can lead to better viewer retention and more predictable viewership patterns, which can positively influence how often your videos are recommended.

Tips to Leverage the Algorithm

Create High-Quality Content: Always aim for quality over quantity. Invest time in creating well-researched, well-edited, and valuable content that viewers will find useful or entertaining. High-quality content tends to have better engagement and longer watch times.

Optimize Metadata: Use relevant keywords in your video titles, descriptions, and tags. This helps YouTube understand what your video is about and match it with viewers interested in that topic. However, avoid keyword stuffing – make sure your metadata is natural and relevant.

Engage with Your Audience: Respond to comments, ask questions, and encourage viewers to like, share, and subscribe. This not only boosts engagement but also builds a community around your channel, which can lead to more loyal viewers and better performance in the algorithm.

Encourage Longer Watch Sessions: Create playlists and link to other videos on your channel to keep viewers watching longer. The more time viewers spend on your channel, the better it is for your overall watch time metric.

Stay Updated: YouTube frequently updates its algorithm and features. Stay informed about these changes by following YouTube's creator blog and community forums. Adapting to new trends and updates can give you an edge over others who might not be as quick to adjust.

CHAPTER 7
Monetizing your YouTube channel

Monetizing your YouTube channel is an exciting step that can turn your passion into a sustainable income stream. Here's a comprehensive guide on how to effectively monetize your content while keeping it genuine and engaging.

Joining the YouTube Partner Program (YPP)

Eligibility Requirements: To join the YPP, your channel needs at least 1,000 subscribers and 4,000 watch hours in the past 12 months. Additionally, you must comply with all of YouTube's policies and guidelines.

Application Process: Once you meet the eligibility criteria, you can apply for the YPP through your YouTube account. The application involves agreeing to the terms and setting up a Google AdSense account to receive payments.

Ad Revenue: As an YPP member, you can earn money through ads displayed on your videos. YouTube places ads before, during, or after your content, and you earn a portion of the revenue based on views and clicks.

Exploring Different Ad Formats

Display Ads: These appear to the right of the video and above the video suggestions list. They are less intrusive and do not interrupt the viewer's experience.

Overlay Ads: Semi-transparent ads that appear on the lower part of your video. They are small and can be easily closed by viewers.

Skippable Video Ads: Ads those viewers can skip after 5 seconds. These ads are popular because they offer the viewer a choice, and you still earn revenue if the viewer watches for a few seconds.

Non-Skippable Video Ads: Ads that must be watched before your video plays. These ads tend to generate higher revenue but can be more intrusive for viewers.

Bumper Ads: Short, non-skippable ads up to 6 seconds long. They are designed to deliver quick, memorable messages.

Leveraging Channel Memberships and Super Chat

Channel Memberships: This feature allows your subscribers to become paying members of your channel. In return, they get perks like exclusive badges, emoji's, and access to members-only content. It's a great way to build a closer community and reward your most dedicated fans.

Super Chat and Super Stickers: During live streams, viewers can purchase Super Chats or Super Stickers to highlight their messages. These features enhance engagement during live interactions and provide an additional revenue stream.

Creating and Selling Merchandise

Merchandise Shelf: If your channel has more than 10,000 subscribers, you can use YouTube's merchandise shelf to showcase and sell your branded merchandise directly below your videos. This integration makes it easy for fans to buy your products.

Custom Merchandise: Consider creating custom merchandise that resonates with your audience, such as T-shirts, hoodies, mugs, and stickers. Use platforms like Tee spring, Merchandise by Amazon, or Painful to handle production and shipping.

Promotional Strategy: Promote your merchandise in your videos, descriptions, and on social media. Share the story behind your products and why they are special to your channel. This personal touch can encourage viewers to make a purchase.

Partnering with Brands

Sponsorships: Brands may approach you for sponsorship deals if your channel aligns with their target audience. Sponsored content involves promoting a brand's product or service in your videos in exchange for payment. Always disclose these partnerships to maintain transparency with your viewers.

Affiliate Marketing: Join affiliates program and promote products that you genuinely use and love. Include affiliate links in your video descriptions and earn a commission for every sale made through your links. Platforms like Amazon Associates and ShareASale are popular choices.

Brand Collaborations: Collaborate with brands to create unique content that benefits both parties. This could be through product reviews, unboxing videos, or tutorials. Ensure the collaboration feels natural and adds value to your viewers.

Offering Exclusive Content and Courses

Exclusive Content: Offer exclusive videos, behind-the-scenes footage, or early access to new content for a fee. Platforms like Patreon allow creators to offer tiered memberships with different levels of access and perks.

Online Courses: If you have expertise in a particular area, consider creating and selling online courses. Share your knowledge through structured lessons and interactive content. Websites like Udemy and Teachable make it easy to create and sell courses.

Workshops and Webinars: Host live workshops or webinars where you can interact directly with your audience. Charge a fee for access and provide valuable, in-depth information on your chosen topic.

Crowdfunding and Donations

Crowdfunding Campaigns: Use platforms like Kickstarter or Indiegogo to fund specific projects or new content series. Explain your vision, set funding goals, and offer rewards to backers.

Direct Donations: Enable donations through platforms like PayPal or Ko-fi. Encourage your viewers to support your channel if they enjoy your content. Many fans are willing to contribute to support their favorite creators.

Tracking and Analyzing Performance

YouTube Analytics: Regularly check your YouTube Analytics to understand which monetization methods are working best for your channel. Pay attention to metrics like revenue, Cost per thousand impressions (CPM), and viewer demographics.

Ad Performance: Analyze which ad formats generate the most revenue and adjust your strategy accordingly. Experiment with different ad placements and formats to find the optimal balance between revenue and viewer experience.

Feedback and Adaptation: Listen to your audience's feedback on monetization strategies. If they feel overwhelmed by ads or promotions, consider dialing back and finding a more viewer-friendly approach. Maintaining a positive viewer experience is key to success long term.

By leveraging these diverse monetization strategies, you can create a sustainable income from your YouTube channel while maintaining authenticity and value for your audience. Remember, building a successful channel takes time and effort, but with dedication and the right approach, you can achieve your financial and creative goals.

CHAPTER 8
Advanced Marketing Tips to Stand Out

Creating high-quality content is just the beginning of a successful YouTube journey. To truly stand out and grow your channel, you need to implement advanced marketing strategies. Here are some tips to help you elevate your YouTube presence:

Optimize Your Video Titles and Descriptions

Crafting Catchy Titles: Your video title is the first thing viewers see. Make it compelling and informative to grab attention. Use power words and create a sense of curiosity without being clickbaity.

SEO-Friendly Descriptions: Write detailed descriptions with relevant keywords to improve your video's search ranking. Include a brief summary of the video, important timestamps, and links to related content or social media. This not only helps with SEO but also provides valuable information to your viewers.

Use Custom Thumbnails

Eye-Catching Design: A custom thumbnail can significantly increase your click-through rate. Use high-quality images, bold text, and bright colors to make your thumbnail stand out.

Consistent Branding: Keep your thumbnail style consistent across your channel to create a recognizable brand. This helps in building a cohesive look and feel, making your videos easily identifiable.

Leverage Social Media

Cross-Promotion: Share your YouTube videos on other social media platforms like Instagram, Twitter, Facebook, and TikTok. Each platform has its unique audience, and cross-promotion helps you reach a wider audience.

Engage with Followers: Interact with your followers on social media by responding to comments, participating in discussions, and sharing behind-the-scenes content. This builds a community around your channel and fosters viewer loyalty.

Collaborate with Other Creators

Find Like-Minded Creators: Collaborating with other YouTubers in your niche can introduce your channel to a new audience. Choose creators whose content complements yours for a mutually beneficial partnership.

Joint Projects: Work on joint projects like guest appearances, co-hosted series, or challenge videos. Promote these collaborations on both channels to maximize exposure and engage both audiences.

Utilize YouTube Analytics

Understand Your Metrics: Regularly review your YouTube Analytics to understand viewer behavior and preferences. Pay attention to metrics like watch time, audience retention, and click-through rates.

Adjust Your Strategy: Use the insights from your analytics to refine your content strategy. If certain videos perform better, analyze why and try to replicate that success in future content. Adjust your thumbnails, titles, and upload times based on what the data tells you.

Engage with Your Audience

Foster Community: Building a strong community is key to long-term success. Respond to comments, ask for viewer feedback, and create content that addresses their questions or interests.

Live Streams and Q&A Sessions: Host live streams or Q&A sessions to interact with your audience in real-time. This helps build a deeper connection and gives viewers a sense of being part of your journey.

Optimize for Watch Time

Engaging Intros: Hook your viewers within the first few seconds of your video to keep them watching. Start with an interesting fact, a question, or a teaser of what's to come.

Structured Content: Organize your content logically and keep it engaging throughout. Use visuals, sound effects, and animations to maintain interest. Encourage viewers to watch until the end by teasing valuable information or a special segment later in the video.

Create Playlists

Organize Your Content: Group related videos into playlists to make it easier for viewers to find and watch multiple videos in one sitting. This not only improves watch time but also helps in better content organization.

SEO Benefits: Playlists are indexed by YouTube and can appear in search results. Use relevant keywords in your playlist titles and descriptions to enhance discoverability.

Consistency is Key

Regular Upload Schedule: Maintain a consistent upload schedule so your audience knows when to expect new content. This helps in building anticipation and routine among your viewers.

Quality over Quantity: While consistency is important, don't sacrifice quality for the sake of frequent uploads. Find a balance that allows you to produce high-quality content regularly.

Invest in Paid Promotion

YouTube Ads: Consider using YouTube ads to promote your channel or specific videos. This can help you reach a broader audience quickly.

Social Media Advertising: Use targeted ads on platforms like Facebook, Instagram, and Twitter to drive traffic to your YouTube channel. Tailor your ad content to the interests and behaviors of your target audience.

Stay consistent, be authentic, and continuously engage with your community to build a successful YouTube channel.

CHAPTER 9
Non-Profit Approach to YouTube Marketing

Taking a non-profit approach to YouTube marketing involves leveraging the platform to promote social causes, raise awareness, and drive positive change. Here's how you can effectively use YouTube to support your non-profit organization's mission:

Telling Compelling Stories

Behind-the-Scenes Content: Give viewers a glimpse into the daily operations of your organization. Show your team in action, whether it's organizing events, distributing aid, or conducting research. This transparency builds trust and engagement.

Testimonials and Interviews: Conduct interviews with beneficiaries, volunteers, and donors. Their personal testimonials can be powerful endorsements of your mission and impact, encouraging others to get involved.

Educating and Raising Awareness

Informative Videos: Create videos that educate your audience about the issues you're tackling. Explain the problem, its causes, and its effects on society. Use data and statistics to back up your points, making the information clear and compelling.

How-To Guides: Offer practical advice on how viewers can contribute to your cause. This could include tips on volunteering, organizing community events, or adopting sustainable practices. Empowering your audience with actionable steps fosters a sense of involvement.

Webinars and Live Streams: Host live webinars and Q&A sessions to discuss relevant topics and engage directly with your audience. Invite experts to share their insights and answer questions. This interactive format can deepen understanding and foster community.

Collaborating with Influencers and Partners

Influencer Partnerships: Collaborate with YouTubers and influencers who share your values and have a substantial following. Their endorsement can amplify your message and reach new audiences. Ensure the partnership feels authentic and aligns with both parties' missions.

Corporate Partnerships: Partner with businesses that support your cause. Co-create content that highlights your joint efforts and the positive outcomes of your collaboration. This can also open up opportunities for funding and resources.

Cross-Promotions: Work with other non-profits or community groups to cross-promote each other's content. This can help expand your reach and foster a network of supportive organizations working towards common goals.

Engaging Your Community

Call-to-Action: Always include clear calls-to-action in your videos. Encourage viewers to donate, volunteer, share your content, or participate in events. Be specific about how they can help and the difference their support makes.

Interactive Content: Use YouTube's interactive features, such as polls, comments, and community posts, to engage with your audience. Ask for their opinions, share updates, and create a dialogue around your cause.

Thank You Videos: Show appreciation to your supporters by creating thank you videos. Acknowledge their contributions and highlight the impact of their support. This fosters a sense of community and encourages continued involvement.

Utilizing Analytics for Improvement

Track Performance: Use YouTube Analytics to monitor the performance of your videos. Pay attention to metrics like watch time, engagement, and audience demographics. Understanding these insights can help you tailor your content to better meet your audience's needs.

Feedback Loop: Encourage viewers to leave feedback in the comments or through surveys. Listen to their suggestions and concerns, and use this feedback to improve your content and strategies.

Adjusting Strategies: Based on your analytics and feedback, adjust your content strategy. Experiment with different video formats, topics, and promotion methods to see what resonates best with your audience.

Promoting Fundraising Campaigns

Fundraising Videos: Create compelling fundraising videos that explain your campaign, its goals, and how the funds will be used. Use storytelling to highlight the urgency and importance of the campaign.

Crowdfunding Integration: Utilize YouTube's fundraising tools, such as the YouTube Giving feature, which allows viewers to donate directly through your channel. Platforms like GoFundMe can also be integrated into your video descriptions.

Event Promotion: Promote fundraising events through your videos. This could include charity runs, auctions, or benefit concerts. Use live streams to cover the events in real-time, making it accessible to a wider audience.

Taking a non-profit approach to YouTube marketing, you can effectively raise awareness, engage your community, and drive positive change. Your content has the power to inspire action, garner support, and make a meaningful impact on the causes you care about.

Chapter 10
Advantages and Disadvantages of Being a Successful YouTuber

Advantages
Creative Freedom:

One of the biggest perks is the creative freedom. You get to create content about topics you're passionate about, experiment with different formats, and express yourself in unique ways. Unlike many traditional jobs, being a YouTuber allows you to follow your creative instincts and see where they lead.

Flexible Schedule:

As a YouTuber, you're your own boss. This means you can set your own schedule, work from anywhere, and take breaks when you need them. Whether you're a night owl or an early bird, you have the flexibility to work at times that suits you best.

Building a Community:

It's incredibly rewarding to build a community around your content. Your subscribers can become a supportive and engaging audience, giving you feedback, sharing your videos, and even forming friendships with each other. The sense of connection and belonging is a huge motivator.

Monetization Opportunities:

Successful YouTubers can make a substantial income through various monetization methods. This includes ad revenue, sponsored content, merchandise sales, and memberships. With dedication and strategic planning, your channel can become a significant source of income.

Personal Growth:

Running a YouTube channel can lead to significant personal growth. You'll learn new skills, such as video editing, graphic design, and public speaking. You'll also develop a thicker skin and learn to handle criticism constructively.

Influence and Impact:

As a successful YouTuber, you have the potential to influence and inspire a large audience. You can raise awareness about important issues, share knowledge, and even make a difference in people's lives. Your platform can be a powerful tool for positive change.

Disadvantages
Inconsistent Income:

One of the biggest challenges is the inconsistency of income. Ad revenue and sponsorship deals can fluctuate, and there's no guarantee of a steady paycheck. This financial uncertainty can be stressful, especially when starting out.

Work-Life Balance:

Maintaining a work-life balance can be difficult. The demands of creating, editing, and promoting content can be overwhelming, leading to long hours and burnout. It's easy to blur the lines between work and personal life when your job revolves around your passions.

Pressure to Constantly Produce:

There's a constant pressure to produce new content. The YouTube algorithm favors regular uploads, which means you need to consistently come up with fresh ideas and execute them. This can lead to creative fatigue and stress.

Public Scrutiny:

Being in the public eye means you're subject to scrutiny and criticism. Negative comments and internet trolls can affect your mental health. It's important to develop a thick skin and learn how to handle criticism constructively.

Algorithm Dependence:

Your success can heavily depend on YouTube's algorithm, which can be unpredictable. Changes in the algorithm can significantly impact your viewership and income. This dependence on an external factor can be frustrating and challenging to navigate.

Privacy Concerns:

Sharing your life online can lead to privacy concerns. As your channel grows, you may find it difficult to maintain boundaries between your public persona and private life. Ensuring your personal information remains secure becomes increasingly important.

Technical Challenges:

Running a YouTube channel requires technical skills and equipment. Learning video editing, understanding SEO, and managing social media can be daunting. Investing in quality equipment can also be expensive.

Isolation:

Working as a YouTuber can be isolating. Unlike a traditional job with colleagues, you might find yourself spending long hours alone, which can affect your social life and mental health. Finding ways to stay connected with friends and other creators is essential.

Despite these challenges, many YouTube find the rewards outweigh the downsides. The key is to approach your YouTube career with realistic expectations, a willingness to learn and adapt, and a strong support system to help you navigate the ups and downs.

Chapter 11
Strategies for Marketing Your YouTube Channel

Social Media Integration

Leverage Multiple Platforms: Share your YouTube videos across all your social media accounts, such as Instagram, Facebook, Twitter, TikTok, and LinkedIn. Each platform has its own audience, so adapting your content to fit each can help you reach a wider audience.

Create Teasers and Previews: Post short teasers or highlights from your videos to pique interest. Use Instagram Stories, Facebook posts, and Twitter tweets to draw attention to your new upload.

Engage Your Followers: Actively engage with your followers by responding to comments, participating in discussions, and sharing relevant content. This builds a community around your channel and encourages your social media followers to check out your YouTube content.

Consistent Branding: Maintain a consistent brand across all platforms. Use the same profile pictures, color schemes, and tone of voice to create a recognizable and professional presence.

Cross-Promotions: Collaborate with other social media influencers or brands to cross-promote content. This can help you tap into new audiences who may be interested in your YouTube channel.

Collaborations and Partnerships

Identify Potential Collaborators: Look for YouTubers or influencers in your niche who have a similar or complementary audience. Collaborations can introduce your channel to their subscribers and vice versa.

Create Engaging Content Together: Plan and create content that benefits both parties. This could be guest appearances, co-hosted videos, or collaborative projects. Ensure that the content is valuable and entertaining for both audiences.

Promote Each Other: Actively promote your collaboration on both channels and across social media. This helps maximize exposure and engagement from both audiences.

Build Long-Term Relationships: Cultivate ongoing relationships with collaborators. Regular partnerships can lead to more opportunities and a stronger community presence.

Networking Events: Attend industry events, conferences and meet ups to network with other creators. Building relationships in person can often lead to more genuine and fruitful collaborations.

Paid Advertising

YouTube Ads: Use YouTube's own advertising platform to promote your videos. True View ads, bumper ads, and pre-roll ads can help increase visibility and attract new viewers.

Social Media Ads: Run targeted ads on platforms like Facebook, Instagram, and Twitter to reach a broader audience. You can create campaigns specifically designed to drive traffic to your YouTube channel.

Google Ads: Leverage Google Ads to promote your videos through search and display networks. This can help your content reach people who are searching for topics related to your niche.

Budget and Targeting: Set a budget for your ads and use targeting options to reach your ideal audience. Demographic targeting, interest targeting, and retargeting are effective ways to ensure your ads are seen by the right people.

Analyze and Adjust: Monitor the performance of your ad campaigns and make adjustments as needed. Analyzing metrics such as click-through rates and conversion rates helps you optimize your strategy and get the most out of your advertising budget.

Community Engagement

Respond to Comments: Take the time to respond to comments on your videos. Engaging with your viewers shows that you value their input and fosters a sense of community.

Host Live Streams: Live streams are a great way to interact with your audience in real-time. Use them for Q&A sessions, behind-the-scenes content, or simply to chat with your subscribers.

Create Community Posts: Use YouTube's Community tab to post updates, polls, and engage with your subscribers outside of video content. This keeps your audience engaged between uploads.

Build a Fan Base: Encourage viewers to subscribe, like, and share your videos. Creating a call-to-action in your videos can prompt viewers to become more involved with your channel.

Recognize Your Viewers: Give shout-outs to loyal subscribers or feature viewer comments in your videos. Recognizing your audience's contributions can build loyalty and encourage more interaction.

Influencer Marketing

Partner with Influencers: Identify influencers in your niche who can promote your channel. Influencers have established trust with their followers, which can be beneficial for attracting new subscribers to your channel.

Product Reviews and Unboxings: If you have a product or service, send it to influencers for review. Unboxing videos and product reviews can drive interest and traffic to your channel.

Affiliate Programs: Create an affiliate program where influencers earn a commission for driving traffic and subscribers to your channel. This incentivizes influencers to promote your content actively.

Authenticity: Ensure that influencer partnerships feel authentic and align with your brand values. Audiences can easily spot inauthentic promotions, which can negatively impact your channel's reputation.

You can effectively grow your channel, reach new audiences, and build a strong, engaged community around your content.

Chapter 12
Content Creation Essentials

Planning and Scripting

Creating compelling content starts with a solid plan. This involves brainstorming video ideas, researching trends, and understanding what your target audience wants to see. Develop a content calendar to organize your ideas and ensure a consistent posting schedule. Scripting is another crucial step. While not all videos need a detailed script, having a clear outline or bullet points can help keep your content focused and engaging. This preparation ensures that your message is clear and that you stay on track during filming.

Filming Techniques

Investing in good equipment can significantly enhance the quality of your videos. While it's possible to start with a smartphone, upgrading to a high-quality camera, microphone, and lighting can make a big difference. Pay attention to your filming environment. A clean, well-lit space can make your videos look more professional. Experiment with different camera angles and shot compositions to keep your visuals interesting. Remember, the goal is to create a visually appealing experience that captures and retains your audience's attention.

Editing Skills

Editing is where your raw footage comes to life. Use editing software like Adobe Premiere Pro, Final Cut Pro, or even free options like DaVinci Resolve. Editing involves cutting out unnecessary parts, adding transitions, and incorporating music and graphics to enhance your video. Pay attention to pacing; a well-edited video should flow smoothly and keep viewers engaged from start to finish. Learning the basics of color correction and sound mixing can also greatly improve the overall quality of your videos.

Being Consistent is Key

One of the most important aspects of content creation is consistency. Posting regularly helps build an audience that knows when to expect new content from you. Consistency also helps with YouTube's algorithm, which favors channels that upload frequently and retain viewers. Create a realistic schedule that you can stick to, whether it's weekly, bi-weekly, or monthly. Consistency doesn't just apply to your posting schedule; it also means maintaining a consistent style and tone across all your videos. This helps establish your brand and makes your channel more recognizable.

Engaging Your Audience

Creating content that resonates with your audience is essential. Encourage viewers to like, comment, and share your videos. Ask questions or create polls to get them involved in your content. Respond to comments and engage with your audience on social media. Building a community around your channel can turn casual viewers into loyal fans. Additionally, consider collaborating with other YouTubers to tap into new audiences and bring fresh perspectives to your channel.

Staying Inspired

Content creation can sometimes feel overwhelming, especially if you hit a creative block. To stay inspired, regularly consume content from other creators within and outside your niche. Look for new trends and ideas that you can incorporate into your channel. Taking breaks and stepping away from your work can also help you return with a fresh perspective. Remember, your passion and enthusiasm will shine through your content and resonate with your audience.

Adapting and Evolving

The digital landscape is constantly changing, and staying relevant means being adaptable. Pay attention to feedback from your audience and be willing to experiment with different types of content. Use YouTube Analytics to understand what works and what doesn't, and adjust your strategy accordingly. Continuously learning and improving your skills will help you grow as a content creator and keeps your channel thriving.

By mastering these content creation essentials, you'll be well on your way to producing high-quality videos that captivate your audience and help you grow your YouTube channel. The journey may be challenging, but with dedication and creativity, the possibilities are endless.

ABOUT THE AUTHOR

My name is Crystal Bowen, a dedicated and motivated individual with a strong work ethic. I thrive on challenges and enjoy collaborating with others. I am 24 years of age. I came from a humble beginning. My journey has taught me the importance of perseverance and determination, driving my life along a positive path. This book is written to guide you on your journey to becoming a successful YouTuber, whether for fun or profit.

www.ingramcontent.com/pod-product-compliance
Lightning Source LLC
Chambersburg PA
CBHW030039230526
45472CB00002B/581